Dear Amy,
wishing to
S

THE AUTHORITY GUIDE TO
MEANINGFUL SUCCESS

How to combine purpose, passion and
promise to create profit for your business

TIM JOHNSON

With Love
Tim xx

The Authority Guide to Meaningful Success

How to combine purpose, passion and promise to create profit for your business

© Tim Johnson

ISBN 978-1-909116-82-5
eISBN 978-1-909116-83-2

Published in 2017 by Authority Guides
authorityguides.co.uk

The right of Tim Johnson to be identified as the author of this work has been asserted by his in accordance with the Copyright, Designs and Patents Act 1988.

A CIP record of this book is available from the British Library.

Printed in the United Kingdom.

Contents

Success without fulfilment is the ultimate
failure.

Tony Robbins

Introduction

There is no shortage of local and global challenges to solve, from climate change, poverty, war and famine, to religious conflict and extremes of wealth distribution to name but a few. Yet we live in a time when we do have the collective know-how and resources to solve most, if not all, of these challenges with relative ease. But why doesn't it happen?

I believe the primary reason is because we've yet to move on from a Darwinian Schumpeterian world of competitive creative destruction in the name of survival of the fittest, to one where we recognise that we are on this planet together and that, despite our different stages of development and world views, we need to progress together… No small task.

Yet the fact remains that the win/lose, winner takes all game is coming to the end of its usefulness, as the excesses of corporate monopolies testify. And the relentless failure of the use of force to solve the world's political and religious differences, which only goes on to reinforce the intractable deadlock for generations ahead, clearly points to the need to approach things differently.

The corporate industrial world has produced all the machines, toys, clothes, films, food – you name it – in abundant supply. It has done this through treating people like machines, with stick and carrot reward systems and executive bonuses through the roof, while at the bottom of the pile, workers work for minimum wage on zero-hour contracts topped up by tax credits (effectively employees subsidised by the state). This system has led to all the stuff we now take for granted, and probably don't want to give up. But it has also left us disconnected from our souls, ourselves, our relationships and our communities. Many feel empty inside and at a time of historical safety and abundance we are stressed out, overwhelmed and disconnected.

Campaigning organisations have sought to redress the destruction brought on by the excesses of corporate greed fuelled by the instantaneous movement of capital, and yet appear to become hamstrung by borrowing corporate models and getting mired in compliance, bureaucracy and political correctness. Worse still, they often embrace the dogmatic right/wrong, win/lose dynamic of the very people they seek to change.

Entrepreneurial organisations use some of the systems of the corporate world but have passion and inspiration as their key drivers; they desire to do things differently for a reason. But they suffer from the lack of access to capital and the ability to run rings around the tax system like the multinational corporations do.

Before grandiose schemes of changing the world, let's first look in our own backyard. It is in smaller organisations that the leaders have the greatest opportunity for change, and to show the efficacy of a new way of working.

Part I

Building an effective organisation

Efficiency is doing things right;
effectiveness is doing the right things.

Peter Drucker

Part I: Building an effective organisation

Regardless of the type or size of an organisation, it needs to have some fundamental cornerstones in order to prosper. Whether a small local business or charity, a religious community, a large multinational corporation, a political party, an education establishment or even a local youth football team, they all need to deal with the following tasks: they need to organise their people to carry out certain jobs, behave in certain ways and to hold certain beliefs; they need to attract people to be members of the team, customers and suppliers; they need to deliver some form of product or service and they need to find a way to finance its activities.

Now in practice, the labels that different organisations use vary greatly. Education establishments talk about teachers or lecturers and students rather than customers or suppliers. Charities talk about fundraising and raising awareness of a cause as opposed to sales and marketing. Religions talk about missionary work and converting people, while political parties trade influence and power.

Whichever labels are used, there needs to be internal systems and processes to allow the people inside the organisation to influence people outside the organisation to interact with it and in some shape or form 'buy' its ideas, products or services.

To reduce this to the fundamental conceptual parts, there are things going on *inside* the organisation and things going on *outside* the organisation. And there are two core processes at large: one of *creating* systems, workflows, procedures, products, services, ideas and so on, and other areas of *connecting* and influencing people to take up these ideas and ways of being.

Which means we have two worlds – an inner world and an outer world; and two core activities of connecting and creating:

Figure 1 The interconnectivity of inside and outside the organisation

Figure 2 The interconnectivity of the two core activities

When we put these four parameters into a grid it looks like the diagram below. The left-hand column is the inner world and the

right-hand column is the outer world; the top row is the activity of connection and the bottom row is the activity of creation.

Figure 3 Outline of the meaningful success map

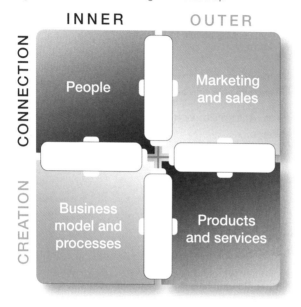

This book is based around the structure provided by this map. It is worth spending a couple of minutes getting familiar with this map and how it links things together. It will make the rest of the book much easier to understand. By the end of the book you'll have a simple framework with which to view your life and your work in a more meaningful and connected way.

Because the map helps to make sense of how everything can fit together so that day-to-day operations can be more easeful and effective, it can enable you to free you and your team up to work beyond the confines of the map and create an organisation that can become a beacon for others to follow.

To give this diagram a little more meaning, the *inner* world of *connection* (the top left quadrant) is the realm of **people** within the organisation, without which there is no organisation, even in a one-man-band set-up.

The bottom left quadrant is what the organisation *creates, internally* to be able to operate; this is its **business model** – how it survives and thrives financially – along with its processes, systems and ways of doing things.

The bottom right quadrant is what the organisation *creates externally*, which is its **products and services** for other people to benefit from.

And finally the top right quadrant is how the organisation *connects externally*, which is the realm of **marketing and sales**.

And if you consider each quadrant as a wheel on a vehicle, then it is important that the wheels are aligned and know where they are going.

Which is why it is so essential to have a crystal clear vision so that each wheel knows where it is heading and can work with the other wheels towards the same aim with the same values.

Creating clarity around vision and values

To start with, it is useful to reassess what business you are in. The classic examples of this are the Ronson (cigarette lighter) and Black and Decker. Ronson had thought they were in the cigarette lighter business, but when they took time out to re-examine what business they were really in, they discovered/decided that they were in the gift-giving business, because people generally bought their products as gifts rather than as utilitarian items. This had a radical impact on the business, as they then changed the whole way they approached the market. Similarly, Black and Decker thought they were in the business of making drills, but when they also examined what business they were in they realised they were in the business of creating holes. This enabled them to focus on projects that DIY people take on, and provide a wide range of solutions to assist with these projects. The shift of focus from looking solely at the products they created, to looking more closely at the customers needs, allowed the businesses to be more innovative with their product designs and solutions, and more focused in their marketing, enabling both businesses to prosper.

Take the time out to re-examine and evaluate what business you are in, particularly with reference to the underlying need that you are fulfilling for your customers. Then define it in a way that allows everyone in your organisation to relate to it as they go about their daily tasks.

Next, be clear about where you are heading – your vision – because you don't want to be like the Grand Old Duke of York, who had ten thousand men, marched them up to the top of the hill and then marched them down again, as the nursery rhyme goes. When I co-founded the business breakfast network, 4Networking, at the very outset the vision was to create a national network. That was it, deliberately simple and clear. That way there could be no ambiguity, no distortion of the message. It was used repeatedly and never changed, until we got there. In the beginning people thought we were mad and that we'd never get there, but the constant repetition and dogged determination towards a very clear goal meant that we did get there. As the organisation grew to thousands of members and remote working team roles of over a thousand people, it was absolutely essential to keep the vision crystal clear, simple to understand and impossible to misinterpret or distort the message. So do the work; what is the clear-cut, simple vision for your business that will see you through the years ahead?

The next thing to get clear about is how you go about doing your work, the culture and values of your organisation. It's not the mechanics at this stage, it's the way you want to behave, the lenses through which you make decisions – the guiding principles. These are your organisation's values. At 4Networking we chose a deliberately relaxed and informal style in contrast to the existing players in the market, and the values of openness, honesty and transparency within the realms of normal commercial expediency.

Returning to the wheels analogy, not only do the wheels need to be directed with a clear vision and values, they also need to be aligned and balanced. Because if the wheels are not aligned and different areas of the business are pulling in different directions, the resulting tug-of-war consumes huge amounts of energy, is unproductive, hard work and wears the tyres out fast. If too much energy is placed on one wheel and the rest of the vehicle can't keep up then wheel-spin occurs, which creates a lot of huff, puff and steam, noise, mess and usually spreads a good deal of muck around in the process. Conversely if one wheel is a little flat or off balance it slows the rest of the vehicle down and creates uncomfortable vibrations for all to feel.

And then there is the drive. Typically younger, more entrepreneurial organisations tend to focus on the people and sales side of things, with the back office set-up and service delivery playing catch-up all the time. In this way, the organisation can be considered to be a front-wheel drive set-up.

More mature businesses and larger charities tend to be run by the accountants and lawyers and focus shifts to efficiency and compliance. Everything is designed to run like clockwork with all the boxes ticked in the right places, and the shift to maximise profits or other metrics can come at the cost of failing to inspire the people in the business and losing sight of the customers' core needs. In this way the organisation can be considered to be a rear-wheel drive set-up.

The key, of course, is to deliberately aim to create a four-wheel drive model where power is distributed to all four wheels, with the ability to adjust the power distribution as the business encounters changes in the marketplace, and deals with the challenges of its own growth. This is where the four connectors, shown in white in Figure 3 (page 5), come in. These will be addressed later in the book, but first let's look at each of the four quadrants or wheels in turn, and some of the key features you need to get right in each of them.

In short

For more meaning – be clear about your values and vision.

For more success – actively create a four-wheel drive approach.

There is a difference between giving directions and giving direction.

Simon Sinek

People

The old adage says 'people are our greatest asset' – and yet how often is this phrase merely lip service? Are your people simply 'human resources' like interchangeable cogs in a machine, or the spirits and souls that drive, shape and propel your organisation forward?

You can have a great brand, products and services, business models, sales and marketing, but unless your people are inspired and enabled to perform, then the impact will be sadly lacking. So how do you do that?

Pick the right people

So often organisations create job descriptions of what they want people to do, then they place adverts for seemingly superhero powers for an average wage. How is that likely to succeed?

A better approach is writing about what types of people like working with you, as that gives a flavour of your culture and the types of people that are attracted to that culture. Then write job scorecards where you look at what the role is meant to achieve, so people can be self-selecting as to whether they are up for the scale of responsibility involved. When hiring, it should be on attitude and cultural fit, rather than an over-reliance on the ability to carry out a certain task. Clearly there are certain specialist roles that require specialist competency, but even then if they can't culturally fit with the organisation's values or if they have a jobsworth attitude, it really is worth continuing the search. One of my early employers also followed the adage of never hiring your second choice candidate; if the first candidate doesn't accept, run the process again. If you have your systems and procedures well honed, then in many cases it should be relatively easy to train someone with the right attitude to learn the task, and you'll have the benefit of them not having to unlearn the way they did things elsewhere.

Teams do well to be balanced and rounded – but individuals do not. While you are looking for an overall consistency of excellence in the running of your company, you'll not get that by hiring consistent, well-rounded people. You'll end up with a lacklustre, beige experience that no one will be passionate about. Hire a mix of people, adapt the role to suit the individual. What is the point of shoehorning people into straitjackets? It's hard work and it creates resistance and payback; it is simply an ineffective way to carry on. And yet that doesn't stop it being common practice.

Hire mavericks, hire tech geeks, hire detail-obsessed admin people and so on. Bring out their individual brilliance, and help them fly in their own area of greatness. Sure it makes things a little harder to manage, because it requires a little thought, compassion, understanding and listening… but when you get it right it's much easier for people to excel and bring the whole energy and effectiveness in the workplace up. Bear in mind the fit between line managers and the people they manage; for example, there is little point having an OCD compliance freak managing an outgoing team of fundraisers.

Leadership and management

Leadership sets the direction, inspires people with the vision, encourages people to come forward with their own ideas towards achieving the vision. Leadership is about enabling, giving people space to make their own mark, to create a culture of can-do and free of blame so that people are not afraid of having a go. Without strong leadership a team will drift, start to create its own agendas and people will simply go and work for an organisation where the leadership is more inspiring.

Having said that, there is inevitably a bunch of sometimes tedious stuff that has to be done in any role and it does need to be managed, measured and accounted for. It is not a case of leadership or management, it is a case of both leadership and management. Both are essential. Ultimately leadership is about inspiring people to the right things, and management is about ensuring they happen effectively and efficiently.

Now you've hired the right people, cross-check that there are not existing people in your team who are actively disruptive or plain dead weight. By all means investigate what might be causing those issues, and we'll look at that shortly, but generally speaking a leopard doesn't change its spots, and if your fish are out of their particular flavour of water, then there is little point in them being there. It is also generally cheaper and certainly much quicker to reach a settlement by means of a compromise agreement, rather than trying to go through the compliance hoops of employment legislation. Trying to complete that process without tripping up is hard enough, it's a management distraction, and it effects everyone else in negative ways too.

Having said that, if people are not performing, it is best to look at your systems, procedures and management practices first. Because let's face it, there is not an exhaustible supply of superheroes out there, and why should you need to be a superhero to get the job done anyway? The aim of the game is to get ordinary people to create extraordinary results, as that really does give competitive advantage – the ability to scale, to be less at the mercy of a few key individuals – and it's a whole lot of fun enabling and watching people preform at levels they previously thought impossible. They love it, and the effect is wonderfully contagious.

So how do you do that? You need to set people up to succeed. That includes leadership (as discussed above) but also a lack of micromanaging. So often in the workplace people are watched like hawks preying on every move in case a mistake is made, which is then quickly pointed out. It's demoralising and ineffective. What you focus on you get more of, so if you focus on where people are underperforming you'll get more underperformance; it's that simple. Focus on what people are doing well, celebrate it, learn from it, amplify it and apply to other people and other areas where appropriate.

But you also need carefully thought-out training, systems and procedures to make it easy to perform well. If you find that your people are trying to bypass the system, it is more than likely that the system is too cumbersome, doesn't do what it should do or they don't understand the need and implications of doing it a particular way. Remember, staff usually don't see the overall picture and tend to look at things from their own perspective. As a leader and manager you need to step into their shoes for a while, engage them in their viewpoints and encourage them to provide ways of improving things. People rarely respond to imposed solutions, and if they're consulted and involved with the problem-solving, they are far more likely to take ownership of the new way of working and provide a much better chance of success.

In short

For more meaning – allow people to bring their spirit and soul to work.

For more success – set people up for success, hire outliers and lead well.

We are a mission-driven company. In order to do this, we have to build a great team. And in order to do that, you need people to know they can make a bunch of money. So we need a business model to make a lot of money.

Mark Zuckerberg

Business model, process and systems

To grow and scale your business or enterprise most people look to sales and marketing as the answer, and obviously it has its place, but in most cases the biggest impact can be made with the business model itself. The big game changers in the marketplace are people with different business models: Uber, the world's largest taxi firm owns no vehicles nor employs its drivers; Facebook, the world's largest publisher owns no content; Alibaba, the world's largest online retailer, owns no inventory. Now, most of us aren't going to be growing global-dominating businesses but the principle remains the same. A small tweak in the business model at the outset with 4Networking meant £30,000 extra net revenue each month down the line – it was the difference between success and failure.

So what can you do differently in your business model?

Where you provide a bespoke service, can this be packaged into products, so they are more standardised? Often there is resistance to such a move, as surely no two cases are the same? But if you look at how there are commonalities in the approach, then I'm sure you'll see a pattern and you can start building from there. The act of looking at how you approach bespoke tasks allows you to see what it is you are actually doing – being consciously aware of what you are doing instinctively – and consequently it becomes easier to establish a process that can be productised and packaged, making it easier to sell and train others to deliver.

The flip side to packaging services into products, is where you provide a product that is usually bought outright like capital equipment or computer software, and consider selling it as a service with a fixed monthly fee under licence.

Be clear about whether you are in a low price, high volume business, or a high price, low volume business. Be clear what the margins are after cost of customer acquisition and whether that makes sense over the lifetime value of the client.

If you do one-to-one work, how can you deliver that work 'one' to many?

If you provide software, for example, can you modularise your building blocks, so you don't have to start from scratch for every project? How could you adapt these concepts to your particular organisation? What changes at the fundamental level of your business could you make? This is important to spend time on, for it is the foundation stone upon which everything else rests. When you have your business model optimised, it primes the pump to allow you to invest in the rest of your organisation.

Processes

Every organisation needs processes in order to operate. Some may be clearly defined and documented, and others may be instinctive and be just because 'that's the way we do things around here.' The challenge is that organisations are rarely static; they change in size and scope, people come and go, and the requirements of the market change, too. This is normal. The issue is that processes are rarely revisited and so 'the way we do things around here' can become cumbersome, as they were devised as stand-alone processes at an earlier time, and as other new processes are introduced the interface and reporting between them can get messy. Processes are a bit like laws made in parliament: there are forever new processes or laws being created, but the old ones stay in place and the whole terrain becomes increasingly complex over time.

When people start bypassing the system to get work done, resist the urge to automatically reprimand the offending person. Ask yourself why is this happening, why is the process so cumbersome that people want to bypass it? What can be done to make the process as simple as possible while ensuring all the necessary value-creating parts are kept in place?

A good way to do this is to give the responsibility of reviewing the individual process to those who use them to ensure they are being reviewed every six months and that recommendations for improvements are produced. They don't have to do all the thinking or decision-making, they just need to be accountable to ensure that a review takes place. By spreading the load widely, no one person has too much to do, and it ensures that the job gets done. A similar approach can be taken with balance sheet items – is it really appropriate for your financial controller to be looking at minor budget items, when these could equally be done by someone closer to the usage?

Systemisation

There is no shortage of software packages out there. The potential issue is that you can end up adapting the organisation to work the way the software was written, rather than the way you want to run the organisation. My take on it is that it is better to run your systems manually at first to get clear on what you want and why, and then you have a much clearer specification to automate. At 4Networking we spent an eye-watering amount of time on a bespoke system that took years to develop as the business grew, but the pain was worth it because it meant we could support a remote team of 1,000 part-time people with a back office staff of just three people.

In-between-ware

If you end up using off-the-shelf software packages, because they already have a lot of functionality built in, are available now and are generally much cheaper than building your own bespoke solution, the problem can be found where the different systems don't interact particularly well with each other. You can to get bespoke 'in-between-ware' software written to help with the interface.

Reporting

The problem with systems is that they can generate masses of reports, and so the call for more and more reporting can grow. It is a problem because in my experience not a lot actually happens or changes as a result of the reports, so the whole activity simply wastes a lot of time and resources.

Spend time working out the key inputs that affect the performance of the outputs that you wish to achieve. What is the minimum dashboard of information with which you can navigate clearly? Having got it down to a minimally-useful dashboard, how can you get that information as close to real time as possible? The profit and loss statement from the accountants is usually not available until several weeks later or more after the operational action that drove the numbers that appear in the accounts – by which time the operational staff are already dealing with the next project. By then people will have forgotten about the causes and papered over any mistakes that may have occurred. The quicker you can get the relevant information, the quicker you can respond, and hopefully the corrections will not need to be knee-jerked; as the old saying goes, 'A stich in time saves nine.'

In short

For more meaning – ensure you only measure the things that matter.

For more success – your business model has the biggest leverage.

Our belief was that if we kept putting great products in front of customers, they would continue to open their wallets.

Steve Jobs

Products and services

The absolute mainstay of your organisation is what you do, your products and services. In many ways it's so obvious and fundamental that it can be easy to overlook giving it due consideration.

What business are you in? It can be very easy to say you are in the business of what you do, such as the baker saying he is in the bread business. But if we look at the underlying need that you serve, a deeper and more meaningful reason may emerge to answer the question of 'what business you are in?' Staying with the example of the baker, the volume produced of sliced white bread is the business's basis of creating strong brand recognition so the consumer consistently repurchases the same product, because of its consistency, ease of use and price. The artisan organic baker, by contrast, is in the business of creating a special experience, a delight in the consumer's mouth with the feel-good factor about investing in the whole experience of consuming a top-quality product that may be five times the price of a standard, sliced white loaf.

So look deeper into the question of what business you are in.

Product life cycle

You may well be familiar with the product life cycle curve that shows the broad phases of introduction, growth, maturity and decline.

Figure 4 Life-cycle curve

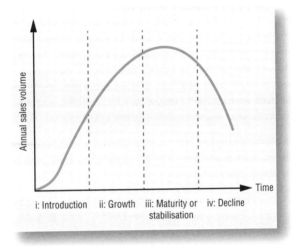

i: Introduction   ii: Growth   iii: Maturity or   iv: Decline
                                    stabilisation

This pattern also holds true for businesses, people, ideas, organisations, cultures, empires and so on!

How is your business affected by the product life cycle? In some industries this is rapid, particularly in technology. The fax machine came and went seemingly in a flash, whereas the bread business is a lot more stable.

Even if you are in a stable industry, such as accounting, the development in technology with cloud-based bookkeeping systems changes the way services are delivered and how value is created. If you don't consciously keep up with developments in the marketplace, then your business may well be heading for the decline stage. Far better to have your eyes open and be an early experimenter with new approaches and leading your sector than playing catch-up all the time.

How broad is your range of products and services? When was the last time you did any analysis on them? Do they all make the same level of profit? Are they all in the same place on the life cycle curve? Are they all as easy to deliver? Which products generate the most customer complaints? The most glowing testimonials? Which are you better at than others? If you created a matrix of all your different customers, and all your different products, and mapped which customers used which products, what would it look like? What would that tell you?

This is not a complete list of questions. The key is to keep questioning. Here is an example of how simply you could map out just two of these questions.

In a profit/product matrix, map out the profit made for each product. Ensure you work out the profit on a similar basis. The working assumptions you have to make in this exercise can be illuminating in itself. For example, how much overhead do you apportion to each product? Is your overhead disproportionately weighted to only delivering some of your products?

Table 1 Profit/product matrix

	Cost of sale	Cost to make	Price sold	Profit
Product A				
Product B				

Product C				
Product D				

In a customer/product matrix, map out which customers buy which products. Could you encourage (with special offers, for example) your existing customers to try more of your products?

Table 2 Customer/product matrix

	Customer 1	Customer 2	Customer 3	Customer 4
Product A	X			X
Product B		X		X
Product C	X			X
Product D			X	X

I recommend that you take time out to do these exercises. Just the mere act of carrying them out will illuminate some blindingly obvious facts, which may cause you to make active decisions.

As a rule of thumb, most organisations have a habit of doing too many things; this happens accidentally with good intent over time. There is always a customer or service user who wants something different from your standard offering. It seems a reasonable request. You can see the potential in growing the business to include that capability and so you do. This process gets repeated often, but not all in the same direction, so the organisation gets pulled and squeezed into different directions at the same time. Over time it means that many organisations become a mishmash of different operations, processes and products. This is suboptimal at best, and the road to oblivion at worst.

It is a highly-competitive market out there, whatever you are doing, and the best way to compete is to be brilliant. One sure-fire way of being brilliant is to do less and to do it well, exceedingly well. Coupled with an unremitting desire and drive for continuous and incremental improvement, you and your team can become unstoppable.

It means that scalability and repeatability become easier, it makes more sense to invest in the system and process development we discussed in the previous chapter, and it means that it becomes easier to occupy a space in the minds of the people in your sector, as we will discover in the next chapter on marketing.

I built two multimillion-pound businesses from start-up using the power of focusing on a single product aimed at a single segment of the market. A super-niching strategy if you will; it is relatively easy to be brilliant in a small, focused area. The wider you spread your focus, the harder it is to become brilliant, and to be known for your brilliance.

Moreover, when you narrow your offering, it gives you the opportunity to collaborate with other players in your marketplace that offer allied services at the boundaries of your offering. If you can develop relationships with other organisations that previously you may have considered competitors, you may be able to find a way of passing a steady stream of work between each other. It has to be worth at least thinking about the next time you're on a long car journey.

One deviation from the single point of focus viewpoint is the notion of the product staircase. This is where introductory products are created that are relatively cheap and high value. They are easier to sell and to acquire new customers with them. This then allows you to establish credibility and trust. Which then makes it easier for your client to purchase the next product because they know, like and trust you, and you've had enough time together to be able to educate the client in the need and value for the next product in the staircase of products.

Some organisations do well with this approach, and it is often trumpeted as the golden panacea. I see its merits, but also make the observation that both my biggest commercial successes were with single-product, single-focus businesses.

In short

For more meaning – understand the real needs your business serves.

For more success – do less and do it brilliantly.

Marketing and sales

When I did my MBA, perhaps the best one-liner I took away was, 'Marketing is the act of going to market.' Now at first glance that may seem a statement of the blindingly obvious, but it's a little more meaningful than that, and I'll use the analogy of a traditional market stall trader to demonstrate.

You see many of us slip into the thinking that marketing is about websites, brochures, the logo and advertising, but it's more than that, much more. The great market stall trader doesn't just set up a pitch and start shouting out the deal of the day, because that can only be done when a whole host of other things has happened in the background. The negotiations and decisions on the stock that is going to be sold, the storage and transport arrangements, before and after, the negotiations with the market itself, where the pitch is and so on, as well as all the legal and financial necessities that all have to be in place in order to operate effectively and sustainably.

So everything that an organisation does should be in support of the act of going to market, otherwise why is the activity being done at all?

This is where the question from the previous chapter, 'What business are you in?' becomes important, because this helps to shape and inform all the activities of the organisation, rather than those that solely focus on promotion and advertising. When the people across the organisation know what business they are in and why, it helps to drive alignment and performance towards a common goal, with shared values about how you approach that.

As a result, there are fewer interdepartmental turf wars and power plays, as alignment around serving the customer in the way the organisation has decided to do it, in the way it does best, becomes the guiding principle. In practice this means delivery drivers enthuse about the business, and pass feedback to sales and marketing. That operational staff are engaged in why they are asked to do things in a certain way because they understand why it is important to the customer. The accounts department is not constantly looking to cut costs as it too understands that delivering quality products, service and customer experience is the key to long-term, sustainable growth and success.

When people in the whole company are committed to their part in marketing, the work becomes more meaningful because they are not just doing things they've been told to do 'because I said so' or because 'that's just the way we do things around here', they understand why this particular function is done in this particular way.

A good example of this principle in action is the charity sector. Charities need to fundraise to generate the income needed to provide their services. In their case, their supporters, can be considered their customers, in addition to the service users, because it is the supporters who are providing the finance to enable the organisation to operate and ultimately prosper. Which is a more nuanced model than the standard commercial model where the service user pays for the products they purchase.

The standard approach in charities is to have separate fundraising teams who generate supporter interest, and everyone else in the charity focuses on their specific roles, whether in service delivery, administration or management. These can be called organisations that fundraise. The problem with this is that supporters only feel valued when they are making donations, and so begin to suffer from donor fatigue, while at the same time the leverage of engaging everyone in the charity is lost.

A far more effective approach is to deliberately create the culture change to create an across-the-board fundraising organisation. The difference here is that all staff in the organisation share the vision, understand the values and how the part they play fits in, and are therefore able to have conversational fundraising exchanges as a normal part of their day-to-day activities. What this means in practice is that supporters are naturally engaged with the activities of the charity and the differences that their contributions are making, so they genuinely feel inclined to continue to actively support the charity. The additional leverage of everyone in the team making a contribution to the core marketing activity of keeping supporters (customers) engaged (happy) compounds the effect in a mutually reinforcing cycle.

Whether you are running a commercial organisation or nonprofit, the principle remains the same: engage your whole team – regardless of role – in the reason you support your customers in the way you do, and train them in how their role is part of that process. There is a classic story illustrating this point. When President John F. Kennedy was making a tour of the NASA facility, he asked a janitor what he was doing and the janitor re-plied, 'I'm helping put a man on the moon, sir.' And so they did!

The strategic view

My take on distilling a marketing strategy, in a nutshell, goes like this.

It's the consideration of a whole range of different factors both within the organisation and in the outside environment as a whole. Through the deliberation of these considerations judgements and decisions are made about how to balance the best fit of the core competencies of the organisation with market demand. At the end of the day, while there are many influences, it is the responsibility of the board of directors or trustees to choose which particular set of decisions they want to make.

The diagram shows a number of the factors that may be considered.

Figure 5 Strategic factors

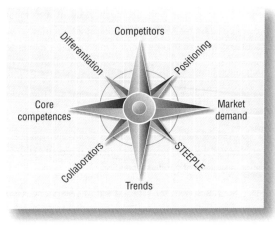

It is generally unwise to attack a competitor head-on as it takes a huge amount of resources and can often fail. While Fuji film reportedly had the mission statement of 'Kill Kodak', which is more of a battle cry than mission statement, Kodak did in fact kill themselves by not adapting to the very digital photography that they ironically invented. The great thing about competitors is that they help to create the market demand for your products and services. When I set up the business breakfast network, 4Networking, we would not have been able to do it so easily had our main competitor not created the market for business breakfast networking in the first place, and provided a continuous stream of disaffected customers that we happily offered a home to. So how can you work strategically with your competitors, so you can all play to your keys strengths, create and strengthen the market between you, but provide subtle differences that allow the people in the market choice?

Positioning is the virtual pigeon hole or filing cabinet that you create over time in the minds of the people who know about you. This is a slow and expensive process, which is why the household brand names hold so much value. It also means that you need to be really clear and consistent about what you are about and why, so you can lock it into people's minds and memories in a soundbite. Everyone has a low attention span and suffers from information overload, so you have to make this as easy as possible for people to assimilate. Repetition, relevance and consistency are key here.

When you collectively consider all the factors in relation to market demand, you will have concluded a thorough, strategic marketing appraisal of your organisation.

STEEPLE is an acronym for a broad set of perspectives from which you can consider the landscape in which you operate.

The perspectives are: *s*ocial, *t*echnological, *e*conomic, *e*nvironmental, *p*olitical, *l*egal and ethical. The idea is simply to be aware of what changes in those areas may affect your organisation now or in the foreseeable future.

Trends are the changes that are happening in your marketplace, and include life cycle issues as discussed in the products and services chapter.

There are collaborators. No person or organisation works in isolation, we have suppliers, customers, introducers and relationships of many kinds just by the act of being in business. Take time out to look at these strategically. Are they the right people? Are there any gaps? Are there opportunities to work more purposefully together rather than by chance on an ad hoc basis? There can be real mileage here, so do take the time to consider this carefully.

Core competencies are the things your organisation is particularly good at; your unique specialisation or assets that are hard to replicate and which set you apart from others in the marketplace. It may be as subtle as having a really clearly-defined, worked through, communicated and lived-by culture that enables you to excel with less staff turnover and far higher productivity per team member.

How are you different? And does that difference matter? Will it stand up against the simple but quite brutal 'so what?' test? There is little point in being different if the difference isn't valuable, or meaningful. Communicate that difference clearly and how it is of benefit so that you start to own that position in the minds of the people in the marketplace.

Tactical marketing

There is a plethora of marketing tactics, but there are some very simple guidelines that are helpful. Many small businesses suffer from *feast and famine cycles* because they stop outwardly marketing when they are busy. When they complete the projects they have, they find they are running out of work and then do a round of promotional activity. Because there is a time delay between promotional activity and the orders coming in, there is a famine phase before they get busy again and repeat the cycle.

The solution to this problem is to be creating awareness and promotional activity in a planned manner so that it happens all the time. If you remember that most of your potential customers or supporters are not in active-buying mode at any one given time, then it easier to understand the necessity of constant marketing communications. It is estimated that people are in buying mode only three per cent of the time, so regular communications that are interesting and valuable will help to keep your brand front of mind when the purchasing decision next comes around.

It is far easier to design a coherent and aligned set of promotional activities when you've carried out the strategic work above.

In short

For more meaning – carry out a thorough marketing strategy review and really nail your underlying 'why?'

For more success – create clear, consistent and compelling marketing communications.

Most organizations are missing this ability
to connect all the data together.

Tim Berners-Lee

Connecting the quadrants

We have been through the four quadrants of the meaningful success map (see Figure 3 on page 5), which was introduced in the chapter, 'Building an effective organisation'. We have looked at the 'big picture', considered core strategies, touched on some tactics in each of the four quadrants, have seen how they are individually essential, and that they need to be aligned and balanced for maximum effectiveness.

In this last chapter of Part I, I'll take you through four connectors that bring power to the quadrants. When you have all four quadrants aligned, balanced and fully connected, that is when things start to take off.

Figure 6 The meaningful success map applied to business

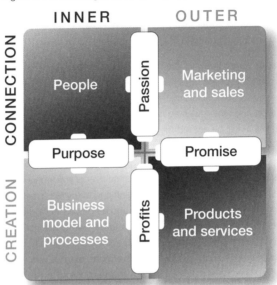

Purpose

Having a great business model, and effective, yet streamlined, processes and systems to support it is essential, (see 'Business model, processes and systems' on page 17). But as the old computer programmers used to say, *GIGO – Garbage In, Garbage Out*. It matters not how great your databases and customer relationship management systems are, if your team doesn't use them properly. Input data needs to be accurate, complete and consistent – and if it isn't, then it won't be long before you are pushing water uphill. Trying to reprimand people for not doing their jobs effectively, basing their bonus payments on the requirement to have used the system for example, may be well intentioned but usually makes resistance to the system greater than it was in the first place. Look to create commitment rather than to control with compliance. Pushing water uphill is hard work and you tend to get wet, so it's best avoided.

Is there a way through this? Yes: be clear about your purpose. The purpose of the organisation, the underlying customer need that you are really fulfilling, the story of the company's vision and mission and why it was so important to the founders, and how that vision will be carried forward. The purpose of the particular department that people are working in and their contribution to the whole, how it fits in and why; the purpose of the particular process or system and how it serves the overall vision. And then down to the individual purpose of each and every team member – how do they relate their life goals and ambitions to working in your organisation? And yes, this should be openly discussed in the appropriate forum and context. Yes, this requires thinking through, and yes, it won't happen overnight, but it is well worth taking the effort to be clear about the purpose of every step. When 4Networking took off, doubling in size year after year, people used to ask me whether I was surprised that it grew so fast. I responded, no not at all, it grew by design; in other words, on purpose!

Passion

'The fish rots from the head' – always. If you are not passionate about your organisation's purpose, its people and your products then forget it, get out, find something else to do because if you can't lead with passion, then no one else will follow with passion. It's as clear-cut as that, plain and simple.

Now it may be that you've inadvertently let things go off the boil and that by implementing the many things suggested in this book you can rekindle your passion and purpose. If that's applicable to you, then I really do hope you do so, as it will transform your life and the lives of many others.

Earl Nightingale once said 'success is the progressive realisation of a worthy goal or ideal', and what is worthy or meaningful is to a large extent whatever we choose to make it. We are meaning creators. So we have a huge influence over what is meaningful. My first successful business was manufacturing specialist cupboard systems for offices, and let's face it, there is nothing intrinsically interesting about cupboards. And yet because of my determination to build a successful business I developed people, systems and products that became the market leaders in their fields, and for me that was an intrinsically meaningful and rewarding thing to do.

Your team members will have different natural passions: some love detail and getting things finished, others love new projects and getting things started, some are fast paced and others more considered. When you can work with people to align their passions within the role they have; it creates an infectious enthusiasm that is difficult to beat.

So passion is a choice. What are you going to choose?

Promise

In order to create meaning between your products and services and your customers, there needs to a psychological contract as well as the formal purchase contract. That's the promise that you and the whole organisation is committed to delivering, time and time again: The thing that your organisation is proud to step up to the plate for, to be known and recognised for, to be determined to deliver and to put right should things falter for any reason.

What's your promise?

Profits

Profits naturally come when your people are engaged and aligned with the culture and vision of the business, and knowing that their role is purposeful with well thought-out processes. When the role is adapted to suit the passions of the individual people and the products and services are excellent so you can consistently deliver on your promises to customers, profits will become sustainable too.

This is a more effective approach than having an accountant-led organisation demanding better performance figures while insisting on budget reductions (do more with less) and in the process demoralising the staff who are meant to be more engaged and enthusiastic to bring about the very same performance improvements.

If you are in a non-profit organisation, re-read profit as 'surplus.' For if you don't create an operating surplus, it is difficult to reinvest in all the things we've discussed so far.

In short

For more meaning – be really clear on purpose throughout the organisation.

For more success – enable a more passionate culture.

The will to win, the desire to succeed, the urge to reach your full potential… these are the keys that will unlock the door to personal excellence.

Confucius

Part II

Enhancing personal effectiveness

To know yourself as the Being underneath
the thinker, the stillness underneath
the mental noise, the love and joy
underneath the pain, is freedom, salvation,
enlightenment.

Eckhart Tolle

Part II: Enhancing personal effectiveness

When we take the four quadrant model of the meaningful success map (see Figure 6 on page 38) and apply it to ourselves personally it looks like this.

The *inner* world of *connection* is the connection with **ourselves**. We all have heard the old adage 'know thyself', and in this quadrant we explore what that really means, and the practical things we can do to get to know, like, love and trust ourselves much more. As we do this, our dependence on the external world becomes far less dominant. And when you reach that pivotal point, everything, and I mean everything, starts to change, and for the better.

The mindfulness people say that when we can create inner peace, it matters not what is happening in the outer world, for we can always find our inner peace. This is the focus of the top left quadrant. (See Figure 7 on the next page.)

The *inner* world coupled with the realm of *creation* is the place where we explore the powerful world of **intention**. Because when we get really clear about our vision, we set the compass point to take us on a journey that allows us to become an improved version of ourselves, we get to experience growth, new experiences, more learning and a whole new world of possibilities.

Figure 7 Outline of the meaningful success map applied personally

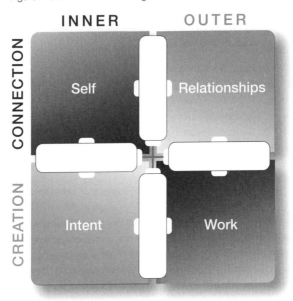

In fact, The Law of Attraction people focus on this quadrant; they purport the mantra, 'Ask, believe and receive.' All we have to do is to get super clear about what we want, create vision boards and the like, and believe that it will happen. That we need not focus on *how* things will happen, but just focus on *what* we want to happen. And trust that it will one day show up for as long as we are open to receiving it – presto all our dreams will come true.

The *outer* world of *creation* is the place of **work**, in whatever form that takes, either conventionally in an organisation, or as a parent, an artist, a truth seeker or whatever activities that make up your external creation. We all know the conventional wisdom of the world of work: work hard at school, get good grades, go to university so you can get a good job, climb the greasy pole of fame and fortune and you will live a satisfied and enjoyable life.

When things at work are going well, we tend to feel better about ourselves generally, though this can lead to an over-reliance and focus on the workplace as the core source of our self-worth. That can have detrimental effects elsewhere in our life and then things can start to unravel. Sadly many conventionally successful people, get 'there' and wonder, 'Is this it?' – they thought they'd be happier when they had achieved their goals.

The *outer* world of *connection* is the space of **relationships**. We all have a myriad of different relationships at different levels, from our primary relationships, to our family and friends, to our work colleagues and the people we mix with at our recreational or sporting meetings, to the relationships with the people in shops, in the street and so forth. We all have them, and the quality of those relationships can have a huge impact on the way we experience life.

There are number of people and organisations that focus on heartful living, who purport that when we learn to transform fear into love and treat everyone accordingly, the whole world becomes a better place. There is something in their wisdom but my take is that they are primarily focusing on the top right quadrant, the place of relationships.

It was in fact through my personal wrestling with all these apparently competing elements that brought me to the creation of this map in the first place, and I originally framed it from the personal perspective. I chose to start this book with a work perspective because that's the practical stuff, the 'how to fix formulae' that everyone expects. But the real juice, the spark, the passion comes in the personal use of this map. When you are, firing on all four cylinders, having a full broadband experience of life, everything else starts to flow so much more easily and you can inspire others to work with the practical stuff in a much more empowering and productive way. This is where success starts to become meaningful.

My original wrestling was with the seeming paradox of happiness being 'out there, when' I had achieved some form of fame and fortune. I'd worked hard to build a successful business, had a car accident, and used the same drive and determination to recover from losing my arm to build another multimillion-pound business. When my relationships with my business partner and then my wife floundered and eventually fell apart, I was left alone renting a flat without out any of the trappings of success that I'd become so accustomed to.

It was an agonising time but it took me on a journey of self-discovery, and hopefully you can benefit from some of the insights from my learnings to enable you to leapfrog ahead without having to take such an extreme path.

I'd chased what I term *conventional success*, the creation of your own flavour of fame and fortune, and discovered to my horror that ultimately it didn't work. While it was nice to have it, it was fickle, it could come and go, and when I had it I was afraid of losing it, and when I didn't have it the sense of grief and loss was palpable.

The first course I did when my life fell apart was a mindfulness course, and with it all the time-honoured Buddhist principles of awareness, acceptance, appreciation and letting go of attachment. Tough, tough schooling for a man who had his own version of 'having it all' – they say 'it's harder for a camel to pass through the eye of a needle than for a rich man to enter into the kingdom of heaven' for a reason!

So if success wasn't out there – on the hamster wheel of always striving for more, and whatever you achieve, never being quite enough – then was it to be found in inner peace? If I could be happy in my own skin regardless of external circumstances, then it didn't matter what the external circumstances were. If that were the case, what was the point of getting out of bed then? I couldn't resolve this seeming paradox. There was no point in working because it's not out there, but if I go for inner peace, then what? How do I live in a modern-day world? I wasn't bold enough to go and live in a monastery on top of a mountain somewhere for the rest of my days.

Eventually it dawned on me that one was about an inner journey and one was about an outer journey. The inner journey was all about connecting with myself, my true essence, and living through the spirit that fires me up; the outer world was the place of creation, the stuff we manifest and make happen.

Those made opposing corners of the soon-to-be-created quadrants, for I then saw how the heart-based work and the law of attraction material all fitted together.

So it's not that these schools of thought are wrong, it's just that they've all got only a part of the picture. When we learn to bring them all together in alignment and harmony, and connect them with the key connectors of Figure 6 (page 38) we saw in Part I, the magic really does begin to flow.

We are brought up in a world where we are encouraged to work hard and achieve a large salary cheque. Then we will be successful, aka happy.

The problem with this approach is we start to assume that success is 'out there, when' – in the future, when external conditions are better. It's a hamster wheel-like trap: there is always another tomorrow, and there is always more to achieve or acquire.

When we learn to feel good inside and radiate our core worthiness, natural spark and vitality, we approach life with an infectious enthusiasm that paradoxically allows us to achieve more externally despite realising external validation is not the path to success.

So let us begin…

In short

For more meaning – take the inner journey.

For more success – bring all four quadrants into the mix.

Meeting ourselves

Most of us go about our daily lives largely on autopilot. Our subconscious mind is wired for survival, and that means if we survived yesterday then doing the same things we did yesterday today makes sense, because if we survived yesterday doing that, then doing the same thing the next day has a good chance of working. The challenge is that we've moved on in evolutionary terms from mere survival to one where we all can truly thrive, and yet we remain hardwired for mere survival.

Moreover, there is so much going on at any one time that, rather than work everything out 'as it is', we are hardwired to pattern match. If something today looks similar to what we have in our memories, then we jump to the nearest pattern to create our own sense out of it. This is great for recognising the infinite types of objects, so we are far better, for example, at recognising all the variations of chairs, or cats, than a computer. The problem comes when we pattern match experiences or situations. When we have had painful or threatening experiences in the past, we can pattern match similarities that are in an entirely different context in the present. So the scary experience that may have been as far back as our childhood can be pattern matched in a fraction of a second to something that feels similar today. This is why we often find that we 'have our buttons pressed' when people 'trigger' certain emotions and responses in us.

The combination of these two traits means that we tend to do just enough to get by and are at the mercy of other people pressing our buttons. This leads to many of us feeling that we are at the mercy of life's events and situations, and consequently we spend a great deal of time, effort and energy trying to control our world so that the circumstances are just right. In this way we feel safe and secure and in control of a predictable life without too many surprises, except occasional ones that break up the monotony!

As the name of the game is to try to control life's circumstance so we don't feel bad, there can be a reinforcing tendency to keep busy doing stuff so that we are occupied or entertained, lest we find ourselves quietening down and having to rest with ourselves and all the uncomfortable thoughts and emotions that may be whirring round in the background at any one time.

Does any of this sound familiar? Would you prefer that other people or events were less of a trigger? Would you like to be at peace with yourself at will? Would you like to discover how to tune into your innate strengths, which are far more powerful than you are probably currently aware?

How it can be

Being still and doing nothing are two completely different things.

Jackie Chan

The key to this is learning to be still, yet wide awake, very alert and aware. Fully alive and yet still. This is entirely different to the ubiquitous zoning out in front of the TV or video game.

I was blessed with a near-death experience following my car accident, and though I didn't recognise the significance at the time, as I didn't see the blinding light, a stairway to heaven or my life flash past me as we are led to believe will happen, the significance later was profound and useful. My experience was that of an empty black infinite space of total nothingness and tranquillity, and what I now recognise as the void. A true space of emptiness and freedom that is ready to receive, from where insights and understandings naturally arise.

Recreating that exact same space while fully conscious isn't easy, but for some people meditation works. I personally go through a bit of a dance with meditation, with it falling in and out of favour. I think it's a vehicle to help you get closer to the void, but it has so many techniques, types and guidelines that it can become confusing and frustrating as the mind tries to work it out. The mind then often gets in the way and ends up deterring the very thing meditation is trying to facilitate. If you've never tried it, there is a great set of meditations in a book in this series, *The Authority Guide to Practical Mindfulness* by Tom Evans. He guides you through ten great, simple, ten-minute meditations that are dead easy to test out.

My take on this is as follows: we live primarily though our thoughts, our emotions and our physical sensations. And the three work in a reinforcing loop together. When we have a series of negative thoughts, our mood starts to drift down and we slouch, which makes us feel worse. We continue to fuel this process by pattern matching similar times, experiences and thoughts and we keep the cycle going until someone or something snaps us out of it.

We can play with this by trying to alter our state by having good physical posture, going out for a walk, forcing ourselves to focus on the positives and remembering some good times to recreate the emotions of happiness. However, in my experience these attempts at state change are often short-lived, but nevertheless a useful part of your personal toolkit.

The trick with a mindfulness-based approach is to step up a level out of the quagmire and simply observe what is going on. This has multiple benefits: when we stand back and observe we can see much more clearly; we are no longer consumed by our emotions but are now able to simply accept, acknowledge and witness them. But, more interestingly, we can also start to tune into the subtler parts of ourselves that are normally drowned out by the mind/body/emotion trio that are running amok most of the time.

When we are still enough to observe and don't make an effort to try and change 'what is', we can also notice not just our thoughts, emotions and physical sensations, but also tune into our sense of soul, that is our core essence, our spirit which is our life force, our intuitions or inner knowings, or more commonly referred to as our 'gut feeling', and the longings of our heart.

When we repeatedly practise doing this, several beneficial things start to develop:

- We become more aware of our thought/emotion/body trio and that awareness gives us the opportunity to lead it rather than to be at the mercy of it. The quicker you notice being aware of the dynamic, the easier it is to shift the dynamic into a direction of your choosing.

- As we learn to practise being witness to our thoughts and feelings we become less afraid of actually experiencing them. This is far more powerful and useful than it may first appear because, let's face it, no matter how bad or terrifying any thought or emotion has ever been, it's never actually killed us or harmed us (in the short term at least). And while President Franklin D. Roosevelt said in his inaugural speech, 'The only thing we have to fear is fear itself', we don't actually have to fear fear, if we can witness it and see it for what it is, which is tremendously freeing.

- As we learn to track our subtler senses, heart, intuition, soul and spirit, we tap into a much more powerful, exciting and capable version of ourselves that is there all the time, but is obscured by the dramas of everyday living.
- When we combine all of these things, we can be less blown about the day's events, get ourselves back on track when they do inevitably give us a nudge, and tap into our own inner power and radiate our natural spark and vitality with infectious enthusiasm outwards from that place rather than hoping external events and people will make us feel better.

The good news is that we are truly responsible for own happiness; the bad news is that we are truly responsible for generating our own happiness as well.

Practicalities with others

You may think it's all well and good me doing this work, but everyone else around me is carrying on the same way, so what good will it do?

When we stop engaging with the dramas that others create, they lose their energy. When you are better able to remain calm in the face of the storm, this becomes settling for others around you. You don't need others to change. As you change, the responses you encounter will naturally adjust, too. Knowing this, too, is tremendously powerful.

In short

For more meaning – listen to more of your being, rather than just your mind.

For more success – rise above the drama and witness what is going on.

Setting goals is the first step in turning the invisible into the visible.

Tony Robbins

Knowing what we want

'Would you tell me, please, which way I ought to go from here?'

'That depends a good deal on where you want to get to,' said the Cat.

'I don't much care where –' said Alice.

'Then it doesn't matter which way you go.'

Alice in Wonderland

Anything that has ever been created by human beings started as a thought, or was developed by a thought following an experience or observation. Our thoughts are incredibly powerful things.

Logic will get you from A to B. Imagination will take you everywhere.

Albert Einstein

You can't do it unless you can imagine it.

George Lucas

To bring anything into your life, imagine that it's already there.

Richard Bach

The true sign of intelligence is not knowledge but imagination.

Albert Einstein

For:

Ideas control the world.

James A. Garfield

And:

Imagination is the true magic carpet.

Norman Vincent Peale

And:

It takes no imagination to live within your means.

Francis Ford Coppola

The lower left-hand quadrant of *internal creation* is the zone (see Figure 7 on page 46) where we use our minds to imagine how we would like to be in the future; where we set our course and **intention** for the journey ahead of us.

How it often is

When you talk with most people you'll most often find that they have ended up in the job or business they are in almost accidentally. It is like the word 'career' is to demonstrate how many of us career all over the place during the 40 or more years we are in the workplace. We change, industries change, curveballs arrive, rarely is it a thought-through linear plan from the onset. It is of course for some, but the 'job for life' is now a thing of folklore.

We tend to settle into our routines by default; we do similar things and behave in similar ways each day, because it is easy and comfortable and our subconscious mind knows it as a strategy to keep us safe. It is very easy to be sucked into a life of comfortable complacency, which at first is wonderful because of the relative lack of stress, but over time becomes dull and uninspiring, and you can be left with the feeling, 'Is this it?' Do I simply exist out my life from now on?

Tony Robbins has a great expression that he used in his 2016 documentary *Tony Robbins: I am not your guru*: that 'life is always happening for us, not to us' for it is easy to get blown about by life's events and think that it is our job to deal with it, manage it and overcome the obstacles as and when they occur. Most people tend to live their lives as if life happens to them, and I certainly know I've spent most of my life like that. But what if we could take an active role in the adventure that lies ahead of us and visualise how we could grow and develop into an evolving version of ourselves that gives us a sense of enthusiasm for living despite the passing years?

A common approach to imagining a better future is to think of all the nice things you want to acquire, like promotions, the ideal partner, houses, cars, holidays, a wardrobe, figure to die for and anything else you care to add. Put these on a vision board and work actively to have them. The challenge is that while this can give you direction, it has two unwanted side effects: first it creates a tension between where you are now and where you want to be. This can make you feel worse than before and demotivated, and consequently you are less able to actually do the work necessary to fulfil your desires. Instead, you may take comfort from a bag of crisps rather than going out for a run. Second, it shifts your thinking to believe that your success and happiness is 'out there, when' you achieve and acquire things. This is a recipe for disaster, for as Plato reminds us, 'The greatest wealth is to live content with little.'

How it can be

The key is not to look for the acquisition of things and experiences to make you feel better, but instead to look for the person you can become so that you can make the most impact and contribution to the areas in life that are important to you, whether that is to your close family and friends, your workplace, your cause or your calling. It's about what's important to you that matters – not what others think.

Use this key to turn things on their head: look at how good you feel when you are doing things well, when you are making a difference, when you light people up by actively appreciating them, or you make someone's day by helping them across the road or give them a great smile at the supermarket checkout. It's realising how good you feel when you give of yourself, rather waiting for external stuff to make you feel good.

So rather than imagining all the stuff you want, use the *Be, Do, Have* model.

How would you like to *Be*? How do you want to show up in the world? What would be a great, authentic expression of yourself, without the need to edit or compromise? It is easy to slip into the stories of our past to think we can't become something, like I can't be a good public speaker or storyteller, or I can't be patient with people, and so on, but this is simply not true. We may well have tendencies to find some ways easier to be than others, either through birth or past experiences, but we can become pretty much who we wish if we are prepared to put the effort in. Timothy Ferris of *The 4-Hour Work Week* fame maintains that through accelerated learning we can all acquire new skills and be in the top five per cent of the people with those skills within a year with dedicated effort.

When you've looked how you'd like to show up and *Be* in the different core areas of your life, what are you going to *Do* differently? What are the habits, routines and rituals you are going to put in place in order to develop the traits and skills that you want to grow into? What are the things you want to *Do* that are going to make the difference that you feel is important?

Finally, when you set the path of how you want to *Be* and what you want to *Do* to become that version of you you've imagined, the things you *Have* will largely take care of themselves. This is because you'll be doing more as a better version of yourself, giving more of yourself and, as a result, you'll inevitably make a bigger impact, which brings its own rewards. Rewards come not just financially but also with the sense of accomplishment and the pleasure of making a difference, too.

So you have a choice: you can let yourself be blown about by life's circumstances and hope you don't get smashed on the rocks, or you can set your compass, raise your sail and learn to navigate the high seas for a great adventure.

In short

For more meaning – imagine how you want to be and enjoy the journey of becoming that version of you.

For more success – develop the disciplines, routines and habits to become the version of you that you imagined.

Discipline is the bridge between goals and accomplishment.

Jim Rohn

Putting it into practice

The bottom right quadrant, the *outer* world of *creation*, is the realm of **work** for most of us (see Figure 7 on page 46). This is where we bring all we've learnt in the book so far and put it into practice. This is where we can transform our own experience of work and create a more enjoyable life for ourselves.

This is meaningful success.

How it often is

The classic dynamic is: do you work to live or live to work?

When we work to live, we can turn up at work, grind it out, play the game, ride the politics and keep our heads down enough to get the monthly pay cheque and be visible enough to be noticed, but not so much that extra responsibilities come our way. When working in this way, time can drag, enthusiasm evades us and we wonder, 'Is this it? Is this what I have go through every day just to pay the bills and keep the roof over our heads?'

Alternatively, those who seemingly live to work can put almost all their energies into the workplace. They work hard, get great results, and they enjoy the positive feedback and affirmation that go with it. As they make a positive impact, the financial rewards follow, they get excited about the future development of the business and how that will further reward them, too. It becomes a self-fuelling dynamic and it can feel great. I've been there. The downside with this approach is that other aspects of their lives may get overlooked; relationships at home and health may be unintended casualties. Divorce is the single most expensive business decision you can make, and the chances are it will be a decision made for you.

And then everything can start to unravel. It did for me and it was an interesting and challenging process, but not for the faint-hearted!

How it can be

It doesn't have to be an either/or choice, where work is either something you endure or absolutely throw yourself into.

We can take elements of both. Work can be a place with personal and financial rewards, the opportunities to create great relationships and to make a difference. But the key is not to attach too much of your self-worth to how you perform at work. You are more than that, and when you do the work on connecting with yourself and relating to others you can balance out the dependence on work as the mainstay of your self-worth.

As a result, the workplace becomes not so much about what you get, but becomes your place of creative expression and self-development, because in fact it is much more about an inner journey than an outer journey.

When you get the inner part right, the external benefits of status and finances will tend to follow more naturally in any event.

You'll then be able to enjoy them more fully, being more appreciative of the choices and freedoms they bring while knowing that they are not the true source of your happiness. You are grounded in your self-assurance, the journey you are on and who you are becoming. This allows your self-belief, confidence and assurance to strengthen. You have a clearer sense of direction and purpose, and greater ability to inspire others and create great works.

In short

For more meaning – use your workplace as a place of authentic creative expression and self-development.

For more success – look at what you can give of yourself, rather than looking at what you can get.

What you get by achieving your goals is not as important as what you become by achieving your goals.

Zig Ziglar

Interacting with others

The top right quadrant of *outer connection* is the realm of **relationships** (see Figure 7 on page 46). Nothing happens in isolation, we are all connected, so it is critical that we get relationships right. When we all get on, everything is so much easier, more fun and more productive. Yet so often there is resistance, judgement and criticism and the atmosphere can become tense, fearful and unproductive. In this chapter we explore why this is so often the case and, more importantly, what we can do about it.

How it often is

The water cooler conversations, the gossip, the pointing out of other people's shortcomings, the arguments, the avoidance, the putting up with the status quo because it's always been like that. This is the way it normally is, the pattern of relating and behaviour becomes established, and once established it tends to become entrenched.

What is the particular flavour of the relating and behaviour in your organisation? All fired up, engaged, supporting, open, productive, creative, blame and gossip free? Or is there a little way to go to get there?

The blame-free culture

I believe no one gets up in the morning and says, 'I'm going to do my best to mess up today, and hide the mistakes I make so the damage they create gets bigger and bigger.' People make mistakes because they are human, because they've other things on their mind, because their motivation isn't as high as it might be; not because they intend to make a mistake. When there is the fear of reprimand and blame, any mistakes made will be covered up and when they are covered up the damage caused by those mistakes grows and the problem is subsequently much harder to fix. When the accusations start to fly, self-defence mechanisms kick in and the available energy to fix the problem is expended finding excuses and other people to blame in order to avoid the heat of the reprimand.

Fear and punishment creates compliance; safety in an open and honest blame-free environment creates commitment. It's your call: as a business or charity leader do you want commitment or compliance?

I was recently asked, 'How do you create that blame-free culture when you have people who constantly blame each other?' and it's a great question, because it is easy to talk about the benefits of having open, clear, blame-free communication, with people owning and taking responsibility for their mistakes and being confident about asking for help when things go wrong or when they get stuck. It's obvious that such a work environment is more productive, more fun to be a part of and more creative. But how do you get there from here?

The first part is acceptance in the way your workplace functions. Map out common patterns of communication, relating and behaviour. What is actually going on? Do this without judgement, or a tendency to edit it in any way. Write down the way it is, as accurately and truthfully as you can. This may be a challenge in itself.

Now give some thought and estimation to the costs in time, money and lost opportunity that this way of working might have. This is an estimate by its very nature, but for example how long does it take to get things done? How much sick leave is there? How much staff turnover is there? How many new and profitable initiatives have come from the base of the organisation? What is the trend of your financial performance? If all these things improved by, say, just 10 per cent, what would the impact of that be?

The next stage is to decide if you want to do anything about that by actively changing the culture. It has to start from the top. Fundamentally, the leaders of the organisation have to decide whether the most effective way is to lead with pressure and with fear or whether can they genuinely see the benefits of inspiring and enabling their teams to perform at a higher level, which can only occur in a blame-free environment.

If the decision is to go ahead, then it starts at the top and is agreed to as a board decision. There needs to be recognition that this is a full-on culture change and that it won't happen overnight. You don't send a memo around and expect behaviour to change. Start by working as a board in a blame-free way. See how challenging it is to open up when you feel vulnerable and afraid. Get used to being supportive of each other and not reacting in a critical way. When discussing issues in the organisation, encourage each other to view things with a constructive lens.

As familiarity of the new way of working is established in the board, the leaders need to start gently shifting the way they lead their line managers. Without fanfare, start talking about the intent to shift the culture and start with one-to-one daily interaction conversations. People have to experience that you mean it and that only comes from actions and not from wishful thinking and grandiose statements. It's when the rubber hits the road; the constant act of not reacting in an accusatory way when things go wrong. People will start to believe when they see it.

When the management of the organisation are on board with this approach, then it is time to be more deliberate about communicating the culture change with the staff, bringing in training where necessary. Again give it time, and lead from the front.

When we developed a blame-free culture at 4Networking, we had a back office team of just three people running the accounts and administration for 600 events a month, with a part-time, remote freelance team of 1,000 people. The back office staff said it was the best job they'd ever had, it didn't feel like work and they actively enjoyed turning up each day. No more working for the weekend, no more Sunday evening blues. In a traditional environment, I estimated we'd have needed to double the back office team; that's how effective this way of working can be.

Building on this

There are three core principles you can use to enhance the development of a blame-free culture: attention, acceptance and appreciation.

Attention

Who likes to be ignored? It's the quickest route to feeling being taken for granted, insignificant and of lesser value. It can be so easy to forget this with the multiple demands that we all face at work, and the pull to be overly task orientated is compelling.

But it doesn't take much to give people a little attention. When you walk around the office, check in with people even if only for a minute or so; look at things from their perspective. Listen! What a treat it can be for some to simply be heard. Give them the gift of actually listening to them without thinking about your response as they are speaking.

Respond to emails, pick up the phone, stay in contact with the people that matter and particularly those in your team, all of them – no exceptions. It can be easy to slip into spending more time with the people you get on more easily with, but in doing so you inadvertently polarise the effect by making it harder to work with the others.

Acceptance

Now this is a little harder! In the workplace there is often the right way of doing things, and if you are anything like I was in my 30s, it was my way and it was right! Management can slip into micromanagement and try to get people doing things in a very particular way, often without reason. People are different, they are not automatons, they are not machines; in fact rename your human resources department, because when you treat them as replaceable component resources you'll not get the commitment you are looking for.

When you can accept people as they are, which from a logical standpoint is the only rational thing to do, for we are who we are and they are who they are, it is simply a statement of fact, then you start to massively reduce any resistance to change. When people feel they are not accepted or not acceptable, then first off they may attempt to adapt their behaviour to fit in, but this is a slippery slope as you are now dealing with someone who is trying to fit in, not feeling their best and certainly not bringing their true, authentic power to their work. Moreover, now that a part of them doesn't feel acceptable, they naturally develop shields of protection, and so as a self-defence mechanism are resistant to change.

Conversely, when you accept people as they are, they can drop their guard a little, you can listen to their concerns and suggestions, you can adapt the role to suit the individual and you can start to foster that individual creative passion in others that we talked about in the earlier chapter 'Connecting the quadrants' on page 37.

When you accept people as they are, you give them a great gift, it reduces conflict and it opens the doorway to a much more productive working relationship.

You may be thinking, 'Yeah right, but so and so simply isn't performing or pulling his weight, so why should I accept them as they are?' Well if this is the case, carrying on being the way you have been clearly isn't working or otherwise the situation would have changed by now. What have you got to lose by trying to accept them the way they are, start an open conversation from that standpoint, and see what happens when over time you engage with their take on things, and you work through the practicalities in a constructive way? If you have a team member that likes to get by through making endless excuses, get into the habit of asking them what they are going to do about it. The flip side of a blame-free culture is the development of personal responsibility, the two go hand in hand, and that's why it is not an overnight fix.

Appreciation

The old adage says, 'what you focus on you get more of', and by and large, it's true. And yet so much management is focused on what is going wrong and how to fix mistakes, and so more mistakes and problems are created. What if you focused on what is going right, acknowledged and appreciated it and focused on facilitating its development and continuation? Not just on the big wins for the high flyers, but the day-to-day little wins that all the staff have. People respond to being appreciated; even if a little British reserve can mean compliments get deflected, they are felt all the same. For many it's such a rare feeling that they'd almost do anything to feel it again. So build it into the culture of your workplace so that it becomes the norm for everyone to become more appreciative in their outlook, both to themselves and to others. It really is the rocket fuel to creating a high performing team.

These principles work equally well in the home as in the workplace, and as more people experience more harmonious relationships at home and at work the compounding and rippling out effect is very powerful.

In short

For more meaning – cultivate the openness required for a blame-free culture.

For more success – actively develop attention, acceptance and appreciation of others.

If you wish to achieve worthwhile things in your personal and career life, you must become a worthwhile person in your own self-development.

Brian Tracy

Connecting the quadrants

At the end of Part I, we discovered the four connectors of purpose, passion and promise to create profits to link the four quadrants together. The four connectors not only do the job of connecting the quadrants, they also add drive and power.

Here we discover how the four connectors bring power to our personal lives, too.

Culture

Culture, as shown in Figure 8 on the next page, connects the world of work and the world of relationships.

Culture is simply the way we do things around here. Normally this is left to default, but as it sets the bedrock of all other behaviours, it really does make sense to consider how you'd like it to be and create a culture deliberately – that is on purpose – by design. This equally applies at home as it does at work. Sometimes we cannot influence the culture of the organisation or club with which we are affiliated, and we are left with a choice of either to be the best we can be within that environment and not submit to the worst aspects or make the choice to leave and find a healthier environment to flourish in. Either way it is worth making a conscious choice as opposed to leaving it to default.

Figure 8 The meaningful success map applied personally

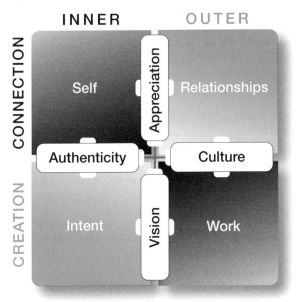

Earlier in the book I discussed the merits of creating a blame-free culture with the underpinnings of self-responsibility, openness, honesty, and with a commitment to a caring and compassionate outlook. That doesn't mean we are all wishy-washy and weak; we can still be energetic, enthusiastic, happening people, but without steamrolling and using undue force and pressure, as it is simply not effective in the long run.

Appreciation

We saw in the previous chapter how the power of appreciation can help to transform relationships, and this is the powerful connector between ourselves and others. It is so easy and natural to notice and gossip about how other people do not meet our expectations and in doing so we flip our focus into criticism. When our focus slips into criticism it affects us in many ways: what we focus on we get more of, so we see more things to be critical of; we become more critical as a person; we become more critical of ourselves; we look for problems rather than solutions and life is a whole lot less enjoyable.

When we keep reminding ourselves to actively appreciate qualities in others and ourselves, we automatically start to bring in the other qualities of attention and acceptance as well. We start to feel better about ourselves, we start to feel better about others, we become a better company and the whole world starts to become a better place.

It may help to reduce your exposure to sources of repeated negativity, such as in mainstream media and the news.

Authenticity

This is the connector between the top left quadrant of *self*, and bottom left quadrant of *intent*. This is the connector between our inner connection with ourselves and creating the clear intent of how we want to be. Authenticity is key here because it is so easy to slip into wanting to be how our partners, peers and parents want us to be or how we perceive society at large wants us to be. We need to be still enough to be able to get below the noise of day-to-day living and the hamster wheel we find ourselves on and listen to the quieter voices that yearn for a different direction or way of being. The way you'd like to be if you had no constraints and could be totally free. How would that be?

Vision

When we've worked out how we'd authentically like to be, we can set out a compelling vision for the way ahead, to experience the type of journey we'd like to have, to learn the skills we'd like to develop to grow into the person we'd like to be, with a great culture of appreciation and authenticity where we and the people around us can thrive rather than merely survive.

In short

For more meaning – tap into your innate self and listen to your authentic longings.

For more success – create a compelling vision.

Meaningful success

The definition of success and what is meaningful for us is individual in nature. Yet the received wisdom that it is 'out there, when' we have achieved goals, attained status and accumulated financial wealth has left many feeling inadequate because they have not achieved those things. Conversely, many people who have achieved those things end up feeling empty because it didn't bring them the happiness they thought it would, and this is often coupled with a fear of losing what they have acquired.

Combining the two parts of this book provides a pathway for you to create a more meaningful version of success for you, and with that it will help you to interact in the workplace with an approach that enables more people to be involved with your vision.

Let's run through the two parts in summary and see how it all fits together. (See Figure 9 on page 81.)

Starting with the personal side first:

1. In the top left-hand corner we saw that when we still our minds and are comfortable in our own skin, we are less controlled by external circumstances and consequently this enables us to develop our self-assurance.

② As we develop our self-assurance we can authentically become clearer about what is important to us and create clear intentions on how we want to be, what we want to do and what we'd like to have.

③ In this way we have a clear vision on how we approach work and what we want our contribution to be.

④ We help to develop a culture at work that is open, honest and blame free and develops self-responsibility. In so doing, we improve our relationships with active appreciation, acceptance and attention.

Which leads on to the *people* quadrant on the top left of the work-based map on the right-hand side.

⑤ People who are aligned with the vision and values of the organisation can approach their work with a clearer sense of purpose and are consequently more committed.

⑥ Which means that when the business model and processes are designed and refined to enable people to succeed, everything becomes more effective and productive.

⑦ As a result, the profits are increased as we move into the products and services quadrant, which are streamlined and focused so they become best in the market.

⑧ Through your organisation's developed excellence you exceed your customers' expectations by consistently delivering on your promises. That creates a positive, reinforcing loop.

In short

For more meaning – look beyond the pay cheque.

For more success – bring your spirit and soul to the workplace, too.

Figure 9 Pathway through the meaningful success map from personal through to business

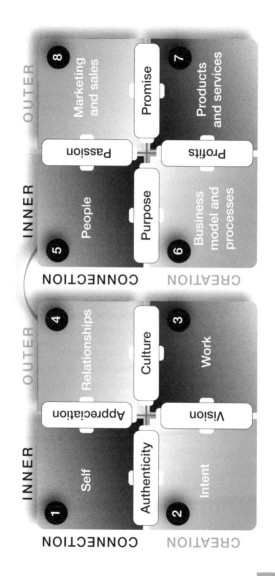

I have wandered all my life, and I have also traveled; the difference between the two being this, that we wander for distraction, but we travel for fulfillment.

Hilaire Belloc

Conclusion

We live in a seemingly mad world, with most of us chasing some form of fame and fortune on the hamster wheel of conventional success 'out there, when'; while others campaign or work to redress the excesses and fall-out of the conventional approach.

But what if we could combine the best elements of both worlds and harness the way commercial organisations mobilise resources effectively, and work in a way that allows people to develop their own natural brilliance? Where we are working for a purpose other than the pay cheque.

If your organisation's focus is deliberately meaningful work like a charity, you may well benefit from entrepreneurial principles to help run your organisation to increase scale and reach without losing the passion for the cause.

If your organisation is more transactional in nature, then looking to the higher purpose of what you are doing, and working with more enabling ways with your team can create a huge increase in personal fulfilment for all involved, as well as the bottom line.

The more this happens, the more the ripple effect makes its impact, because happier and fulfilled business leaders create happier families and that radiates and compounds. As these business leaders develop the people in their organisations, so they too go home and create more harmonious relations in their families. They interact with their colleagues, customers and suppliers similarly, and the ripple effect continues. As the efficacy of working this way becomes more apparent, other organisations will follow suit, and so the ripple effect continues.

Eventually this leads to less disaffected people, less conflict and anxiety, better communication and the possibility to use the freed-up energy to solve the long list of challenges we all face as a whole.

Is that worth getting out of bed for?

What are you going to do differently now?

About the author

After coming from a background in engineering and manufacturing, Tim Johnson took a fledgling start-up to become a multi-million-pound turnover, market-leading business. While making cupboard systems was not intrinsically rewarding in itself, Tim created meaning with an unremitting pursuit of improvement in product quality and service delivery, and in the process created direct employment for 50 people.

Following a car crash in 2001, Tim lost his arm and had to sell the shares in his business. The near-death experience, physical recovery, emotional healing and mental training on the Bristol MBA programme helped Tim broaden his skill set and deepen his resilience.

He went on to co-found the business breakfast networking organisation, 4Networking, to support the growth of micro-businesses. Tim co-created the 4N-Way, which combined culture, processes and progress through the organisation to lead members on a pathway to success. The result was the rapid growth of the business from nothing to 300 groups and thousands of members in a few short years.

When the compromises in his relationships with his wife and business partners became too great to bear, they unravelled, eventually leading Tim to lose it all and to take two years out on a journey of self-recovery, research and reflection culminating in the writing of the best-selling business book, *The Success Book: How to grow yourself and your business*.

Tim now helps business and charity leaders to develop their teams and organisations with the principles of meaningful success. He is also an acclaimed public speaker and inspires audiences to see that they can do far more than they currently believe.

meaningfulsuccess.co.uk

Other Authority Guides

The Authority Guide to
Emotional Resilience in Business:
Strategies to manage stress and weather
storms in the workplace

Robin Hills

How do your challenges inside and outside of work impact upon your emotions and your resilience?

The emotional resilience of those involved in a business will contribute significantly to the organisation's success. This *Authority Guide* from leading emotional intelligence expert, Robin Hills, will help you change the way you think about yourself and the way you approach potentially difficult situations. You will be able to develop your own personal resilience and understand how to develop resilience within the hearts and minds of your team and your organisation.

The Authority Guide to
Practical Mindfulness:
How to improve your productivity,
creativity and focus by slowing down for
just 10 minutes a day

Tom Evans

Enhance your wellbeing, creativity and vitality with mindfulness meditation.

In this *Authority Guide*, Tom Evans, invites you to embrace the benefits of meditation in both your life and your business. With the practical mindfulness meditative techniques described in this book, you will learn how to get more done in less time. You will discover how to generate ideas off the top of your head and how to allow serendipity to land at your feet. This book opens the door to a new way to be and do.

The Authority Guide to Mindful Leadership: Simple techniques and exercises to manage yourself, manage others and effect change

Palma Michel

How do you implement mindfulness in the workplace?

Today's leaders and organisations need to develop an agile mindset and take bold risks. This *Authority Guide* shows you how to link mindfulness directly to leadership and business challenges and offers practical and accessible tools for change. Written by an expert on leadership, meditation and mindfulness, the book teaches you how to manage your inner landscape of thoughts, emotions and interruptions so that you can create a compassionate, innovative and sustainable working culture.

We hope that you've enjoyed reading this *Authority Guide*. Titles in this series are designed to offer highly practical and easily-accessible advice on a range of business, leadership and management issues.

We're always looking for new authors. If you're an expert in your field and are interested in working with us, we'd be delighted to hear from you. Please contact us at commissioning@suerichardson.co.uk and tell us about your idea for an *Authority Guide*.